Under Your Skin: Your Amazing Body

Mick Manning
and Brita Granström

Albert Whitman & Company, Morton Grove, Illinois

Contents

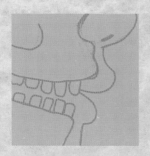
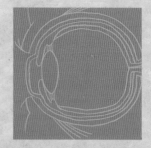

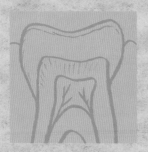

Welcome to your body!

Would you like to know how your own body works? Well, this book is all about *your* body, inside and out—so read on. Flip the flaps and sneak a look at what's happening under your skin!

BRAINS ARE BOSSY!

Let's start with your brain. It's inside your head and always bosses your body around! It tells your lips to smile, your eyelids to blink, your nose to twitch . . .

In fact, your brain has just made an order: open this book! That told the nerves to move some muscles that moved bones that moved your fingers to open the book and turn the page.

Now it's going to give your body another order: "Flip the flap and look inside your head."

HEAD

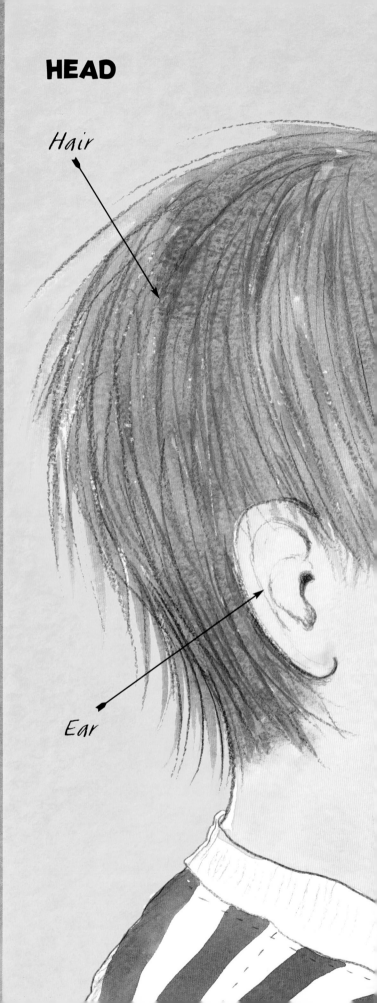

Hair

Ear

Your brain weighs about the same as a pet rabbit! It is jelly-soft but protected by your bony skull.

Spinal cord

NERVES

Nerves link different parts of your body to your brain. They look almost like plant roots getting finer and finer as they branch out.

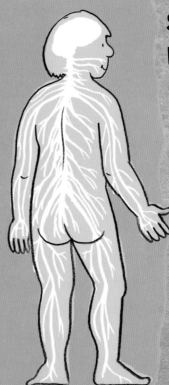

SENDING MESSAGES

Messages travel along these nerves to and from the spinal cord, a long nerve bundle that runs up your spine (backbone) to your brain.

LEARNING

Every time you learn something, a new nerve path is made inside your brain. The more you experience something, the better these new nerve paths get! It's like a weedy path that gets clearer and clearer every time your thoughts "walk" there!

5

Smell it!
See it!

SIGHT

Eyes let you see the world you live in. They face forward, both looking at the same object at the same time, but from slightly different positions. That helps you judge distances—useful when catching a ball.

Some people's eyes don't work very well—wearing glasses can help. Glasses have plastic (or glass) lenses for you to look through. Your eyes have lenses, too; flip the flap and see!

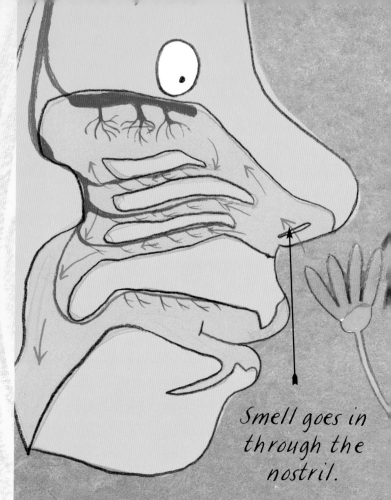

Smell goes in through the nostril.

SMELL

You smell when you sniff air into the higher part of your nose. Here, there are nerves covered with tiny hairs and mucus (you call it snot). The nerves sample the air and send messages up to your brain, which can recognize smells—or learn new ones.

Want to look inside my eye?

EYES

A round eye muscle (the iris) adjusts the size of the black hole at its center (the pupil). It makes the hole bigger or smaller so the right amount of light shines through the lens. Then the lens focuses this light on the back of your eye, the retina. It's almost like a movie screen, but the picture is upside-down!

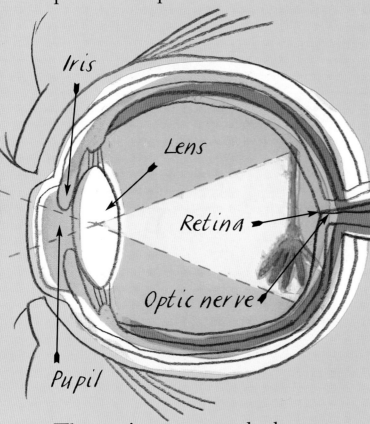

Iris

Lens

Retina

Optic nerve

Pupil

The optic nerve sends the upside-down picture to your brain, which turns the image right-side-up!

What color are your eyes? It's the iris that gives them their color.

Brown

Green

Blue

Touch it! Taste it! Hear it!

TOUCH

When you touch something, you feel it with your sensitive fingertips. Nerves send messages to your brain explaining the sensation— it may be rough or smooth, lumpy or wet, hot or cold . . .

TASTE

Your tongue is a sloppy taste machine! It's covered with taste buds that each pick up different tastes— salty, sweet, bitter, and sour. Try some taste sensations. Lick a salty chip and then a sour lemon —blagh!

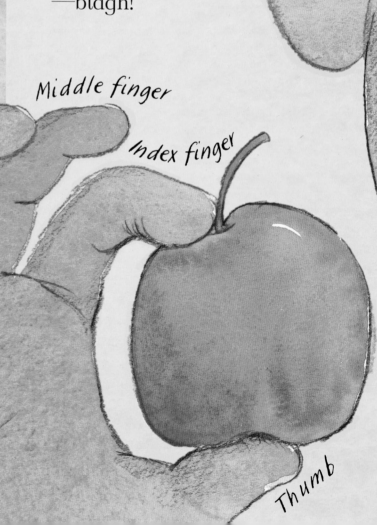

Little finger

Ring finger

Middle finger

Index finger

Thumb

All flavors are a mixture of your four taste sensations.

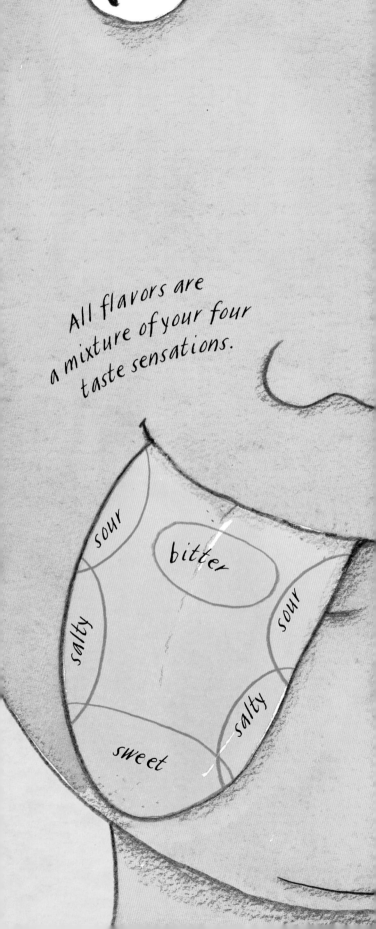

HEARING

Your ear flap catches sound as it moves through the air and funnels it into your ear hole. The sound hits your eardrum, a tightly stretched piece of skin, and makes it vibrate like a drum.

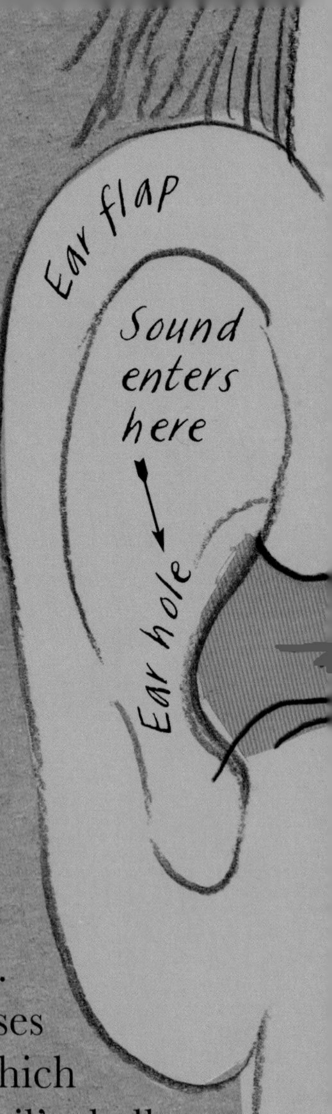

Tiny bones in the middle ear vibrate. This vibration passes to the inner ear, which is shaped like a snail's shell and is filled with liquid.

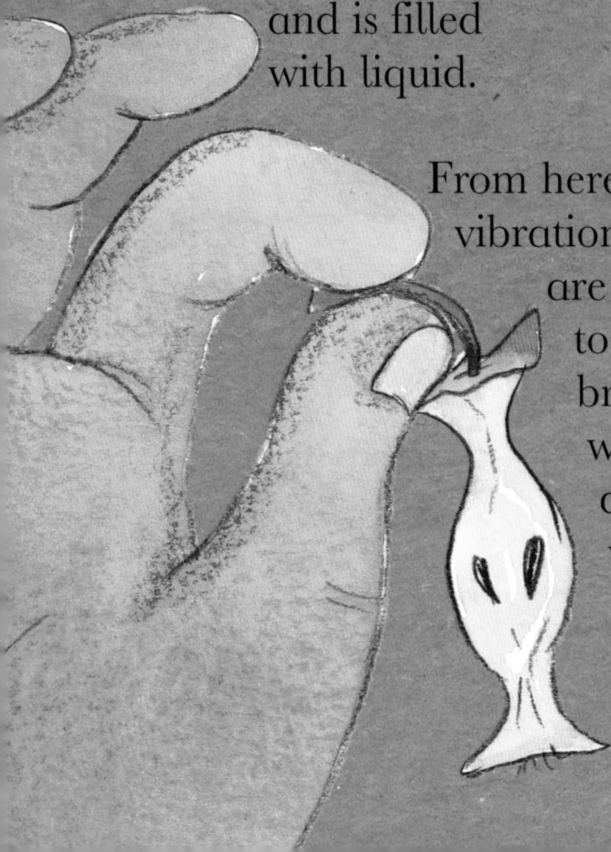

From here, the vibrations are sent to the brain, which decides what sounds they are.

Ear flap

Sound enters here

Ear hole

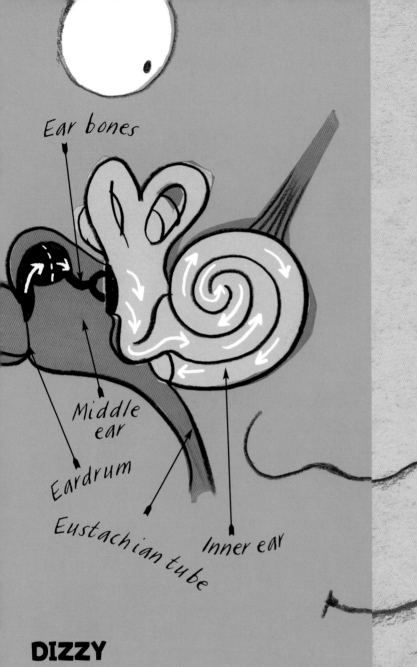

Ear bones

Middle ear

Eardrum

Eustachian tube

Inner ear

POP
Your ears pop sometimes when you're in a car or plane because of sudden changes in the air pressing on the Eustachian tube. The tube keeps the air pressure the same inside your ear as it is outside.

HARD OF HEARING
Some people have a hard time hearing—it can help if they wear a small speaker in their ear called a hearing aid.

DIZZY
The inner ear helps you balance. The liquid in it warns your brain about any movement. If you spin round quickly, all the movement signals confuse your brain. You get dizzy and fall over!

I taste my apple and hear it go crunch!

On the move!

SKELETON

From long leg bones to tiny ear bones, bones are hard, strong, and grow with you. You have 206 bones that fit together to make your skeleton. This is your body's framework—without it you'd be like a wibbly, wobbly jellyfish! Joints connect your bones and allow you to move.

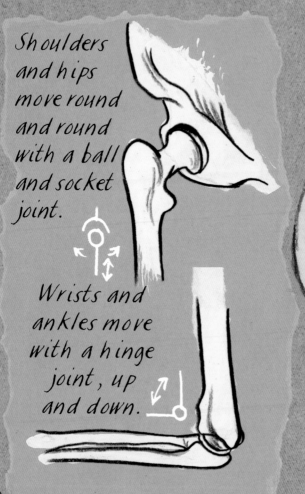

Shoulders and hips move round and round with a ball and socket joint.

Wrists and ankles move with a hinge joint, up and down.

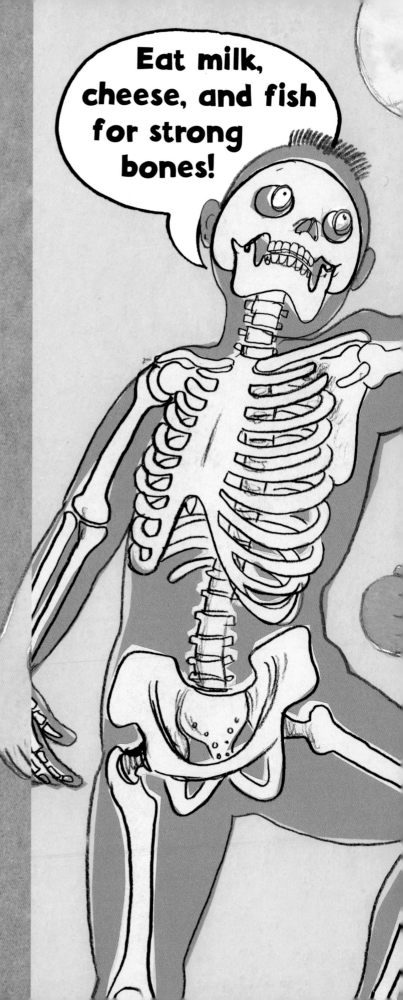

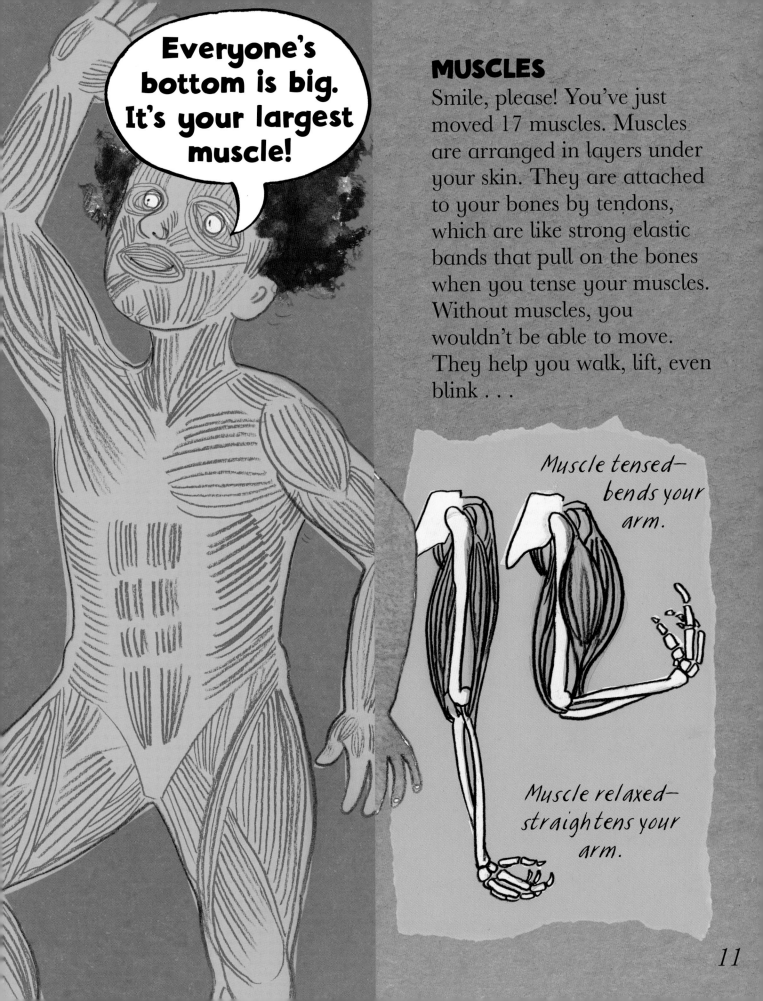

Everyone's bottom is big. It's your largest muscle!

MUSCLES

Smile, please! You've just moved 17 muscles. Muscles are arranged in layers under your skin. They are attached to your bones by tendons, which are like strong elastic bands that pull on the bones when you tense your muscles. Without muscles, you wouldn't be able to move. They help you walk, lift, even blink . . .

Muscle tensed—bends your arm.

Muscle relaxed—straightens your arm.

11

Hair, voice, and teeth

HAIR

Hair keeps you warm. It grows almost everywhere on your body. Hair is growing all the time—that's why you need haircuts. Some hairs fall out, but new ones grow. Sometimes, as adults grow older, hair stops growing, leaving bald spots.

Hair roots grow in tubes in your skin called follicles.

Sweat gland (see page 20)

Nerve

Follicle

VOICE

You can speak because of your vocal cords. These are flaps inside your throat. When you speak, air from your lungs makes the vocal cords vibrate, and this creates sound. The vocal cords are tightened or relaxed as different sounds are made.

Vocal cord

Cross-section

These sounds go up your throat and come out of your mouth, but they need your teeth and tongue to turn them into words . . .

Throat

Vocal cords

Windpipe

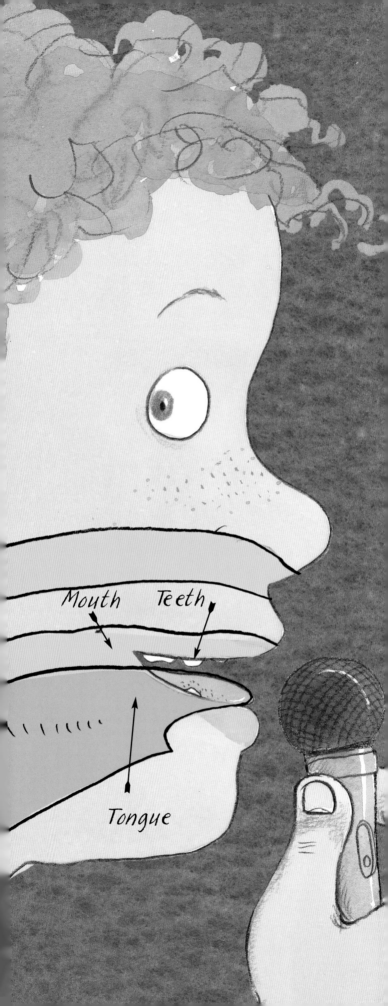

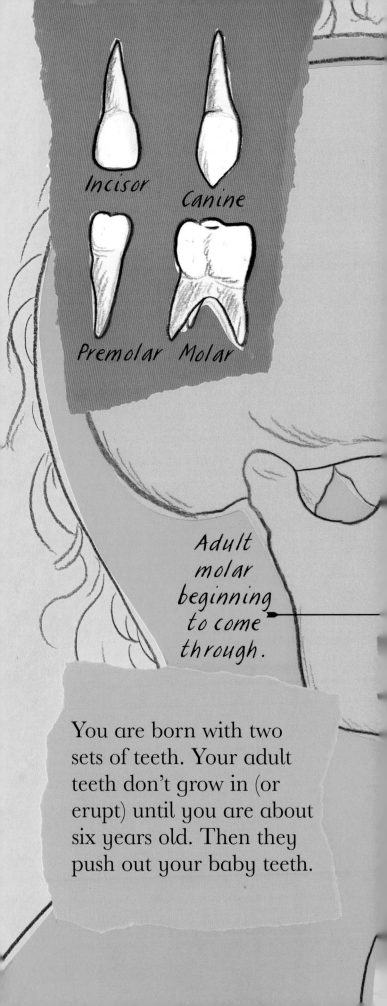

Incisor

Canine

Premolar Molar

Adult molar beginning to come through.

You are born with two sets of teeth. Your adult teeth don't grow in (or erupt) until you are about six years old. Then they push out your baby teeth.

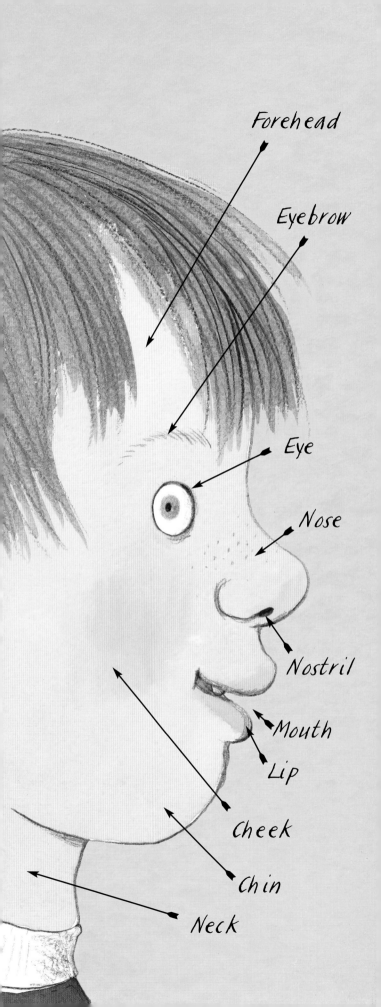

Forehead

Eyebrow

Eye

Nose

Nostril

Mouth

Lip

Cheek

Chin

Neck

INSIDE THE HEAD

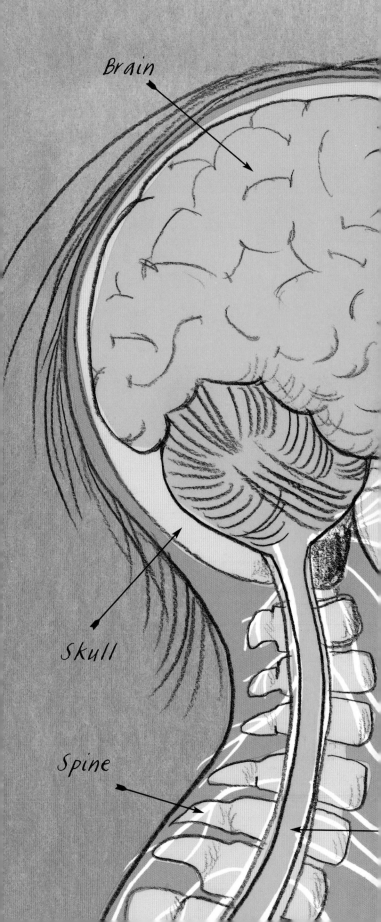

Brain

Skull

Spine

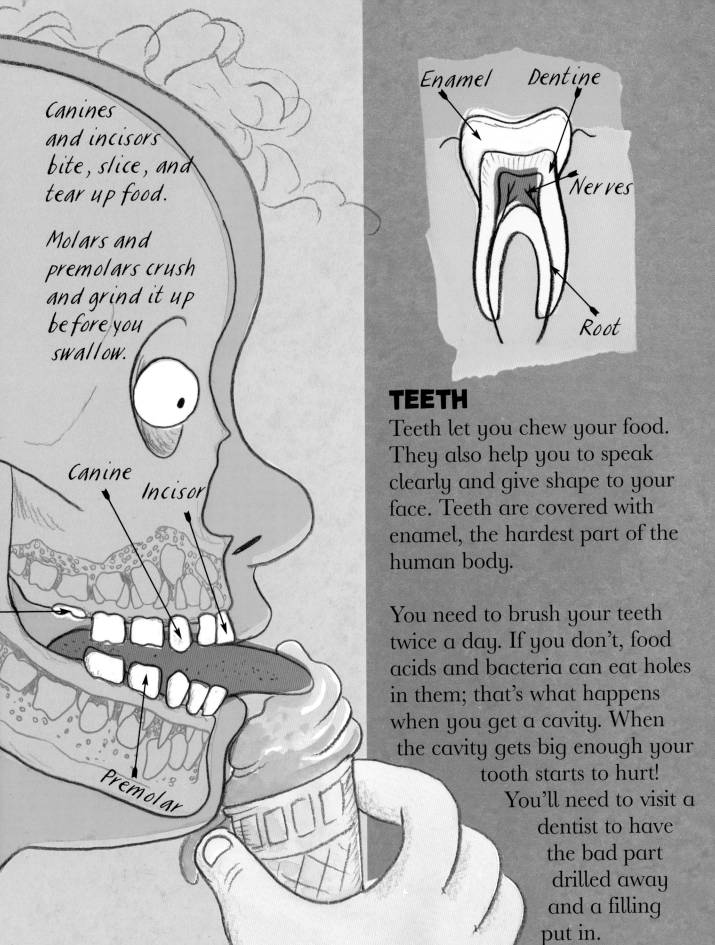

Canines and incisors bite, slice, and tear up food.

Molars and premolars crush and grind it up before you swallow.

Canine

Incisor

Premolar

Enamel   Dentine

Nerves

Root

TEETH

Teeth let you chew your food. They also help you to speak clearly and give shape to your face. Teeth are covered with enamel, the hardest part of the human body.

You need to brush your teeth twice a day. If you don't, food acids and bacteria can eat holes in them; that's what happens when you get a cavity. When the cavity gets big enough your tooth starts to hurt! You'll need to visit a dentist to have the bad part drilled away and a filling put in.

Rumbly tummy

You must eat and drink to stay healthy. Food contains the fuel that your body needs to work, but your body has to digest food (liquefy it) to take out the fuel. Every time you swallow food, you are sending it on a long journey through your digestive system, which starts in your mouth and ends in the bathroom.

CHEWING

Your mouth is like a food blender! When you chew, your teeth and tongue break food up and mix it with saliva, which starts to dissolve it.

GULP

When you swallow your food, it goes down your throat and into your food pipe. This muscly tube squeezes your food down to your stomach.

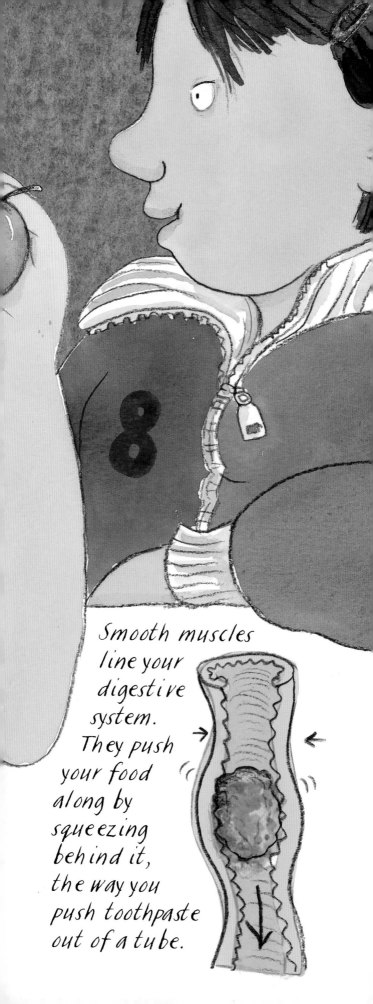

Smooth muscles line your digestive system. They push your food along by squeezing behind it, the way you push toothpaste out of a tube.

THE TUMMY

Your food goes down your food pipe to your tummy, or stomach. Your stomach is a stretchy sack that breaks down your food with digestive juices to turn your food into a thick soup.

INTESTINES

Then, the soup is squeezed through your intestines—which are over twenty feet long! Here, your food is broken down so that all of the stuff your body needs can be put into your blood and carried all around your body.

OUT THE END

Your rectum is your body's own trash can! All the lumpy waste from the food you have digested collects there. Next, it's squeezed out as poop. Waste liquid is stored in a bag called the bladder and when it is full, it comes out as pee.

) Tongue—pushes food down he throat.

) Epiglottis—a flap that shuts off our windpipe, the way to your lungs, hen you swallow.

) Food pipe—squeezes your food own to your stomach.

) Stomach—digests and makes your ood a liquid.

) Liver—creates a fluid called bile, hich helps digest fat.

) Pancreas—makes digestive juices.

) Small intestine—breaks down food o that all of the nutrients you need an pass into your blood.

) Large intestine—absorbs water and reates waste from the parts of food our body can't use.

) Rectum—stores lumpy waste until ou dump it.

Feel your heartbeat!

Your blood is constantly moving around your body. It's pumped along by a muscle that never stops working—your heart. You hear and feel it as a heartbeat. Feel your blood pumping through your body by gently pressing your fingers to the vein on the back of your wrist. What you feel on your wrist is called your pulse.

Your pulse is the stretching of the arteries caused by blood surging through your body each time your heart beats.

I'm getting in shape!

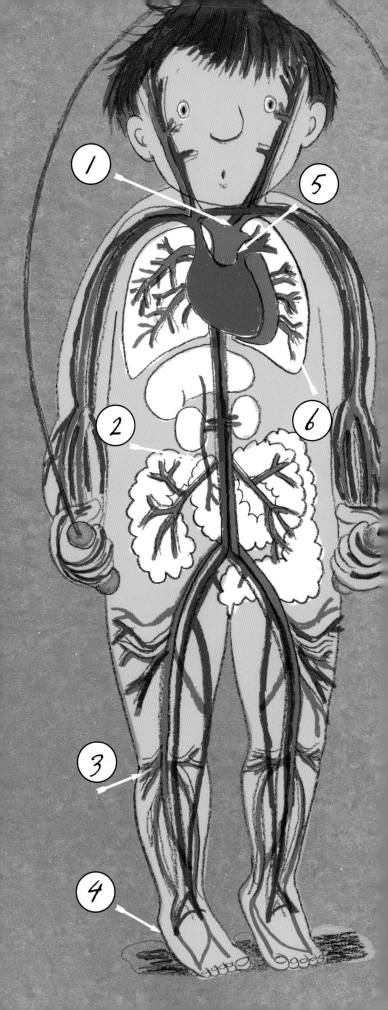

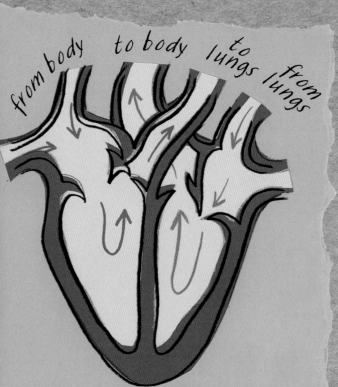

from body   to body   to lungs   from lungs

Blood goes through your heart twice on each journey round the body.

CIRCULATION

Blood's journey around the body is called circulation because the blood always comes back to your heart. Your blood moves through tiny tubes called vessels (arteries and veins). Imagine these are like a train track, and the blood is the train, dropping off and picking up passengers on its way around the body.

ROUND AND ROUND

1 Bright red blood leaves the heart down the main artery. Full of oxygen from the lungs, it moves into smaller arteries that branch out over your body.

2 The blood picks up the nutrients in your food from the intestines. (See page 15)

3 Oxygen and fuel pass out of the blood into the body. Waste passes back in, including carbon dioxide.

4 The blood is now dark red (blue in the diagram). It pushes into veins which take it back to the heart.

5 Next, the pulmonary arteries take the blood to the lungs to unload carbon dioxide and load up with new oxygen.

6 Now the blood is bright red again, ready to go through the body once more.

IN THE BLOOD

Some of the passengers your blood carries include nutrients from your food (your body's fuel) and the oxygen from the air. Your body uses the oxygen to burn up the fuel, which gives you the energy to live. This makes wastes, including carbon dioxide—another passenger for the blood to carry away!

Blood is made of liquid called plasma. The plasma in your blood picks up and collects fuel and waste, but it also carries millions of tiny particles with other jobs to do.

Red cells carry oxygen to all parts of the body.

White cells are your body's defending army, attacking germs inside your body.

Platelets stick together to make clots to stop a cut from bleeding.

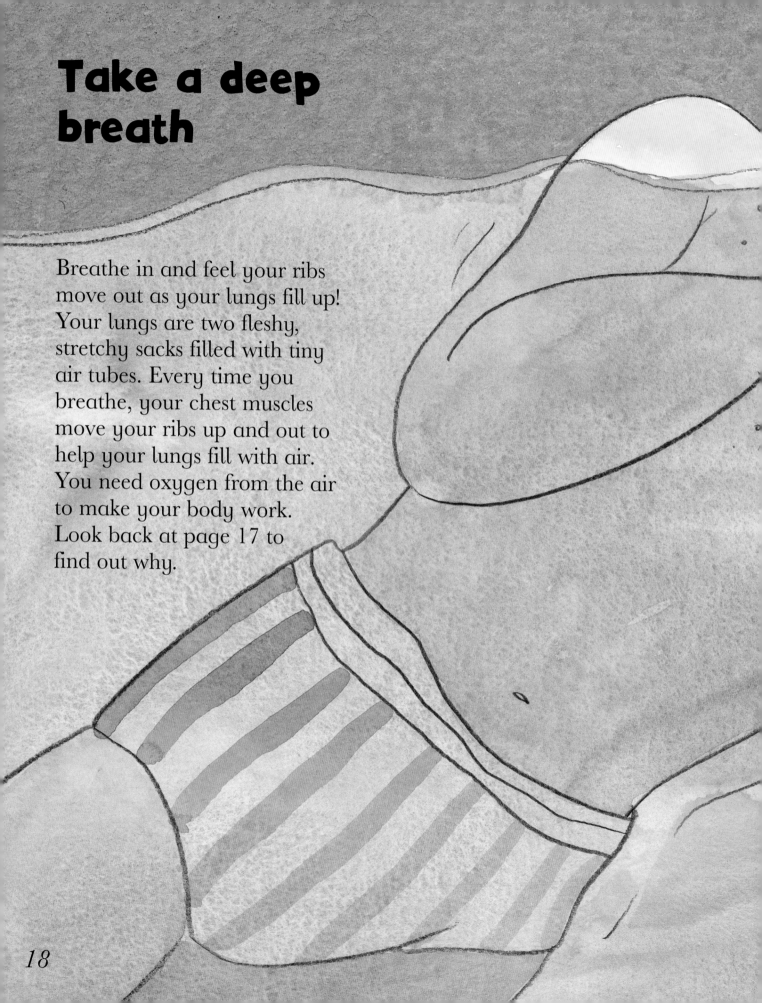

Take a deep breath

Breathe in and feel your ribs
move out as your lungs fill up!
Your lungs are two fleshy,
stretchy sacks filled with tiny
air tubes. Every time you
breathe, your chest muscles
move your ribs up and out to
help your lungs fill with air.
You need oxygen from the air
to make your body work.
Look back at page 17 to
find out why.

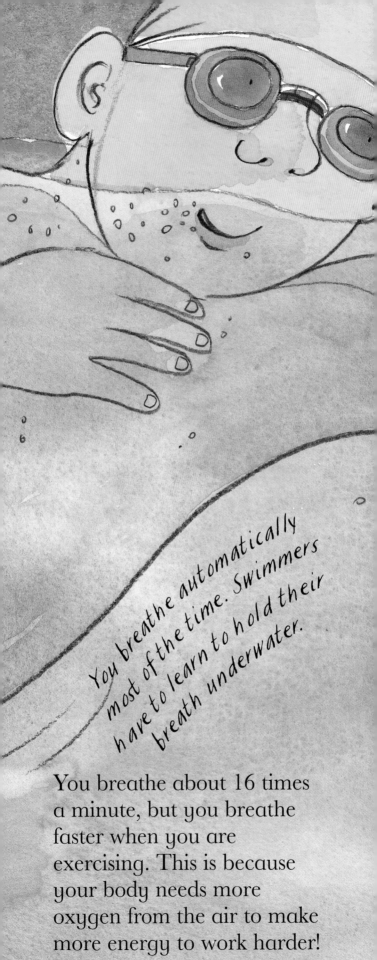

You breathe automatically most of the time. Swimmers have to learn to hold their breath underwater.

You breathe about 16 times a minute, but you breathe faster when you are exercising. This is because your body needs more oxygen from the air to make more energy to work harder!

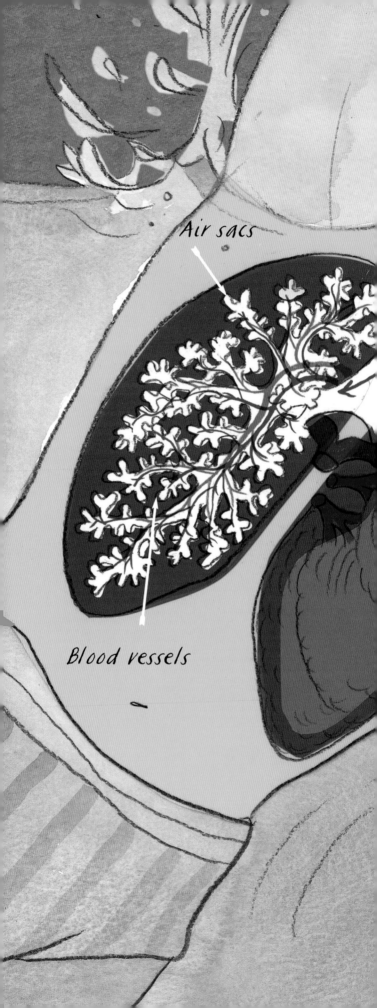

Air sacs

Blood vessels

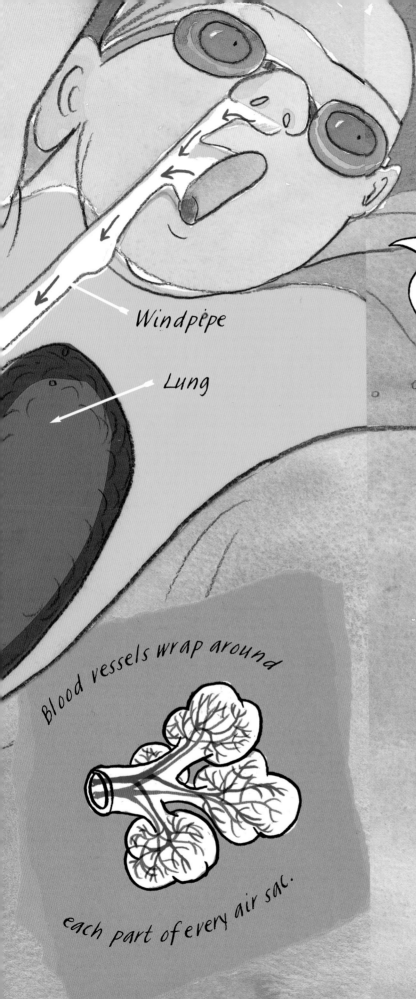

INTO THE LUNGS

When you breathe, air goes down your windpipe into the two air bags we call your lungs.

Windpipe

Lung

Don't forget to breathe!

Blood vessels wrap around each part of every air sac.

BRANCHING OUT

Inside the lungs, the air tubes branch out, getting smaller and smaller until they end in tiny air sacs, which are wrapped in blood vessels. The oxygen passes into the blood to be pumped round the body by your heart.

OUT AGAIN

While oxygen passes into the tiny blood vessels, waste carbon dioxide passes out of them, back into the lungs to be breathed out in your next breath.

19

Skin-tight

The final layer of your body is the one you see—your skin. Skin is amazing. It's a waterproof, stretchy covering that fits you like a glove.

Your skin contains blood vessels, nerves, glands, and hair roots (see page 12). Skin also has tiny holes in it, called pores. When you get hot, the pores open to let out waste water called sweat. As the sweat dries off, it takes away some of your body's heat and cools you down.

Sweat keeps you cool but it can also make you smell bad, so you need to wash it off!

Slap on the sunblock!

SKIN COLOR

Skin contains melanin. This is a pigment that acts like a filter to protect skin from the sun's dangerous rays. People whose ancestors come from hot, sunny countries have more melanin in their skin—and the more they have, the darker their skin. This is why people come in all sorts of colors!

However much melanin your skin has, it still needs protection from the hot sun. Make sure you use sunblock lotion.

MAKING DUST

Tiny pieces of skin flake off your body all the time. They form a lot of the house dust we sweep up! But don't worry, skin always replaces itself. Even when you cut or scrape yourself, new skin grows back.

Bodies are wonderful

So now you can say, "I've seen inside my body!" But let's just remind that bossy brain of yours one more time about all the wonderful things everybody's body can do.

Ears hear sounds—and your brain enjoys them.

Eyes see words—and the brain learns to make sense of them.

Bones help us stand, walk, run, and play.

Noses smell everything—and the brain remembers the sweet and the stinky.

Muscles lift, pull, push, and let us wiggle.

Hair is always growing.

Blood fights germs—even babies can fight off disease.

Our digestive system turns food into body fuel.

Lungs are always breathing.

Hearts tick like watches—about 70 beats a minute.

New skin grows, and old skin becomes house dust!

Index

For Max, Björn and Frej with love, Mum and Dad

Library of Congress Cataloging-in-Publication Data

Manning, Mick.
Under your skin : your amazing body / written and illustrated by Mick Manning and Brita Granström.
p. cm.
Originally published: My body book. London : Franklin Watts, 2006.
  ISBN 10: 0-8075-8313-8 (hardcover)
  ISBN 13: 978-0-8075-8313-5 (hardcover)
    1. Human physiology—Juvenile literature.
    2. Toy and movable books. I. Granström, Brita.
    II. Title.
      QP37.M347 2007
      612—dc22
      2007002350

Published in 2007 by Albert Whitman & Company, 6340 Oakton Street, Morton Grove, Illinois, 60053-2723. Published simultaneously in Canada by Fitzhenry & Whiteside, Markham, Ontario. All rights reserved. No part of this book may be reproduced or transmitted in any form or by any means, electronic or mechanical, including photocopying, recording, or by any information storage and retrieval system, without permission in writing from the publisher. Printed in China.

10 9 8 7 6 5 4 3 2 1

Find out more about Mick and Brita at www.mickandbrita.com.

For more information about Albert Whitman & Company, please visit our web site at www.albertwhitman.com.

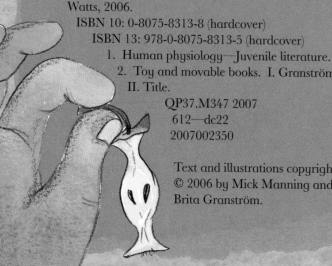